DOOR INTO THE DARK

SEAMUS HEANEY

Door into the Dark

faber and faber
LONDON · BOSTON

First published in 1969
by Faber and Faber Limited
3 Queen Square London WC1N 3AU
Reprinted 1969 and 1974
First published in this edition 1972
Reprinted 1977, 1981, 1985 and 1988

Printed in Great Britain by
Redwood Burn Limited, Trowbridge, Wiltshire
All right reserved

ISBN 0 571 10126 7 (Faber Paperbacks)
ISBN 0 571 08998 4 (hard bound edition)

For my father and mother

CONTENTS

ACKNOWLEDGEMENTS

Acknowledgements are due to the editors of
the following magazines, in which some of
these poems have appeared:
*The Dublin Magazine, The Honest Ulsterman,
The Irish Press, The Irish Times, The Listener,
New Statesman, Outposts, Phoenix, Times
Literary Supplement, University Review*; and
to the Northern Ireland Service of the B.B.C.
Some details in "Requiem for the Croppies"
are taken from P. O'Kelly's "General
History of the Rebellion of 1798",
Dublin, 1842.

NIGHT-PIECE

Must you know it again?
Dull pounding through hay,
The uneasy whinny.

A sponge lip drawn off each separate tooth.
Opalescent haunch,
Muscle and hoof

Bundled under the roof.

GONE

Green froth that lathered each end
Of the shining bit
Is a cobweb of grass-dust.
The sweaty twist of the bellyband
Has stiffened, cold in the hand
And pads of the blinkers
Bulge through the ticking.
Reins, chains and traces
Droop in a tangle.

His hot reek is lost.
The place is old in his must.

He cleared in a hurry
Clad only in shods
Leaving this stable unmade.

DREAM

With a billhook
Whose head was hand-forged and heavy
I was hacking a stalk
Thick as a telegraph pole.
My sleeves were rolled
And the air fanned cool past my arms
As I swung and buried the blade,
Then laboured to work it unstuck.

The next stroke
Found a man's head under the hook.
Before I woke
I heard the steel stop
In the bone of the brow.

THE OUTLAW

Kelly's kept an unlicensed bull, well away
From the road: you risked fine but had to pay

The normal fee if cows were serviced there.
Once I dragged a nervous Friesian on a tether

Down a lane of alder, shaggy with catkin,
Down to the shed the bull was kept in.

I gave Old Kelly the clammy silver, though why
I could not guess. He grunted a curt 'Go by

Get up on that gate'. And from my lofty station
I watched the business-like conception.

The door, unbolted, whacked back against the wall.
The illegal sire fumbled from his stall

Unhurried as an old steam engine shunting.
He circled, snored and nosed. No hectic panting,

Just the unfussy ease of a good tradesman;
Then an awkward, unexpected jump, and

His knobbled forelegs straddling her flank,
He slammed life home, impassive as a tank,

Dropping off like a tipped-up load of sand.
'She'll do,' said Kelly and tapped his ash-plant

Across her hindquarters. 'If not, bring her back.'
I walked ahead of her, the rope now slack

While Kelly whooped and prodded his outlaw
Who, in his own time, resumed the dark, the straw.

THE SALMON FISHER
TO THE SALMON

The ridged lip set upstream, you flail
Inland again, your exile in the sea
Unconditionally cancelled by the pull
    Of your home water's gravity.

And I stand in the centre, casting.
The river cramming under me reflects
Slung gaff and net and a white wrist flicking
    Flies well-dressed with tint and fleck.

Walton thought garden worms, perfumed
By oil crushed from dark ivy berries
The lure that took you best, but here you come
    To grief through hunger in your eyes.

Ripples arrowing beyond me,
The current strumming water up my leg,
Involved in water's choreography
    I go, like you, by gleam and drag

And will strike when you strike, to kill.
We're both annihilated on the fly.
You can't resist a gullet full of steel.
    I will turn home fish-smelling, scaly.

THE FORGE

All I know is a door into the dark.
Outside, old axles and iron hoops rusting;
Inside, the hammered anvil's short-pitched ring,
The unpredictable fantail of sparks
Or hiss when a new shoe toughens in water.
The anvil must be somewhere in the centre,
Horned as a unicorn, at one end square,
Set there immoveable: an altar
Where he expends himself in shape and music.
Sometimes, leather-aproned, hairs in his nose,
He leans out on the jamb, recalls a clatter
Of hoofs where traffic is flashing in rows;
Then grunts and goes in, with a slam and flick
To beat real iron out, to work the bellows.

THATCHER

Bespoke for weeks, he turned up some morning
Unexpectedly, his bicycle slung
With a light ladder and a bag of knives.
He eyed the old rigging, poked at the eaves,

Opened and handled sheaves of lashed wheat-straw.
Next, the bundled rods: hazel and willow
Were flicked for weight, twisted in case they'd snap.
It seemed he spent the morning warming up:

Then fixed the ladder, laid out well honed blades
And snipped at straw and sharpened ends of rods
That, bent in two, made a white-pronged staple
For pinning down his world, handful by handful.

Couchant for days on sods above the rafters
He shaved and flushed the butts, stitched all together
Into a sloped honeycomb, a stubble patch,
And left them gaping at his Midas touch.

THE PENINSULA

When you have nothing more to say, just drive
For a day all round the peninsula.
The sky is tall as over a runway,
The land without marks so you will not arrive

But pass through, though always skirting landfall.
At dusk, horizons drink down sea and hill,
The ploughed field swallows the whitewashed gable
And you're in the dark again. Now recall

The glazed foreshore and silhouetted log,
That rock where breakers shredded into rags,
The leggy birds stilted on their own legs,
Islands riding themselves out into the fog

And drive back home, still with nothing to say
Except that now you will uncode all landscapes
By this: things founded clean on their own shapes,
Water and ground in their extremity.

IN GALLARUS ORATORY

You can still feel the community pack
This place: it's like going into a turfstack,
A core of old dark walled up with stone
A yard thick. When you're in it alone
You might have dropped, a reduced creature
To the heart of the globe. No worshipper
Would leap up to his God off this floor.

Founded there like heroes in a barrow
They sought themselves in the eye of their King
Under the black weight of their own breathing.
And how he smiled on them as out they came,
The sea a censer, and the grass a flame.

GIRLS BATHING,
GALWAY 1965

The swell foams where they float and crawl,
A catherine wheel of arm and hand;
Each head bobs curtly as a football.
The yelps are faint here on the strand.

No milk-limbed Venus ever rose
Miraculous on this western shore.
A pirate queen in battle clothes
Is our sterner myth. The breakers pour

Themselves into themselves, the years
Shuttle through space invisibly.
Where crests unfurl like creamy beer
The queen's clothes melt into the sea

And generations sighing in
The salt suds where the wave has crashed
Labour in fear of flesh and sin
For the time has been accomplished

As through the shallows in swimsuits,
Bare-legged, smooth-shouldered and long-backed
They wade ashore with skips and shouts.
So Venus comes, matter-of-fact.

REQUIEM FOR THE CROPPIES

The pockets of our great coats full of barley—
No kitchens on the run, no striking camp—
We moved quick and sudden in our own country.
The priest lay behind ditches with the tramp.
A people, hardly marching—on the hike—
We found new tactics happening each day:
We'd cut through reins and rider with the pike
And stampede cattle into infantry,
Then retreat through hedges where cavalry must be
    thrown.
Until, on Vinegar Hill, the fatal conclave.
Terraced thousands died, shaking scythes at cannon.
The hillside blushed, soaked in our broken wave.
They buried us without shroud or coffin
And in August the barley grew up out of the grave.

RITE OF SPRING

So winter closed its fist
And got it stuck in the pump.
The plunger froze up a lump

In its throat, ice founding itself
Upon iron. The handle
Paralysed at an angle.

Then the twisting of wheat straw
Into ropes, lapping them tight
Round stem and snout, then a light

That sent the pump up in flame.
It cooled, we lifted her latch,
Her entrance was wet, and she came.

UNDINE

He slashed the briars, shovelled up grey silt
To give me right of way in my own drains
And I ran quick for him, cleaned out my rust.

He halted, saw me finally disrobed,
Running clear, with apparent unconcern.
Then he walked by me. I rippled and I churned

Where ditches intersected near the river
Until he dug a spade deep in my flank
And took me to him. I swallowed his trench

Gratefully, dispersing myself for love
Down in his roots, climbing his brassy grain—
But once he knew my welcome, I alone

Could give him subtle increase and reflection.
He explored me so completely, each limb
Lost its cold freedom. Human, warmed to him.

THE WIFE'S TALE

When I had spread it all on linen cloth
Under the hedge, I called them over.
The hum and gulp of the thresher ran down
And the big belt slewed to a standstill, straw
Hanging undelivered in the jaws.
There was such quiet that I heard their boots
Crunching the stubble twenty yards away.

He lay down and said 'Give these fellows theirs.
I'm in no hurry,' plucking grass in handfuls
And tossing it in the air. 'That looks well.'
(He nodded at my white cloth on the grass.)
'I declare a woman could lay out a field
Though boys like us have little call for cloths.'
He winked, then watched me as I poured a cup
And buttered the thick slices that he likes.
'It's threshing better than I thought, and mind
It's good clean seed. Away over there and look.'
Always this inspection has to be made
Even when I don't know what to look for.

But I ran my hand in the half-filled bags
Hooked to the slots. It was hard as shot,
Innumerable and cool. The bags gaped
Where the chutes ran back to the stilled drum
And forks were stuck at angles in the ground

As javelins might mark lost battlefields.
I moved between them back across the stubble.

They lay in the ring of their own crusts and dregs
Smoking and saying nothing. 'There's good yield,
Isn't there?'—as proud as if he were the land itself—
'Enough for crushing and for sowing both.'
And that was it. I'd come and he had shown me
So I belonged no further to the work.
I gathered cups and folded up the cloth
And went. But they still kept their ease
Spread out, unbuttoned, grateful, under the trees.

MOTHER

As I work at the pump, the wind heavy
With spits of rain is fraying
The rope of water I'm pumping.
It pays itself out like air's afterbirth
At each gulp of the plunger.

I am tired of the feeding of stock.
Each evening I labour this handle
Half an hour at a time, the cows
Guzzling at bowls in the byre.
Before I have topped up the level
They lower it down.

They've trailed in again by the readymade gate
He stuck into the fence: a jingling bedhead
Wired up between posts. It's on its last legs.
It does not jingle for joy any more.

I am tired of walking about with this plunger
Inside me. God, he plays like a young calf
Gone wild on a rope.
Lying or standing won't settle these capers,
This gulp in my well.

O when I am a gate for myself
Let such wind fray my waters
As scarfs my skirt through my thighs,
Stuffs air down my throat.

CANA REVISITED

No round-shouldered pitchers here, no stewards
To supervise consumption or supplies
And water locked behind the taps implies
No expectation of miraculous words.

But in the bone-hooped womb, rising like yeast,
Virtue intact is waiting to be shown,
The consecration wondrous (being their own)
As when the water reddened at the feast.

ELEGY FOR A STILL-BORN CHILD

I

Your mother walks light as an empty creel
Unlearning the intimate nudge and pull

Your trussed-up weight of seed-flesh and bone-curd
Had insisted on. That evicted world

Contracts round its history, its scar.
Doomsday struck when your collapsed sphere

Extinguished itself in our atmosphere,
Your mother heavy with the lightness in her.

II

For six months you stayed cartographer
Charting my friend from husband towards father.

He guessed a globe behind your steady mound.
Then the pole fell, shooting star, into the ground.

III

On lonely journeys I think of it all,
Birth of death, exhumation for burial,

A wreath of small clothes, a memorial pram,
And parents reaching for a phantom limb.

I drive by remote control on this bare road
Under a drizzling sky, a circling rook,

Past mountain fields, full to the brim with cloud,
White waves riding home on a wintry lough.

VICTORIAN GUITAR

For David Hammond

*Inscribed 'Belonged to Louisa Catherine Coe before
her marriage to John Charles Smith, March 1852.'*

I expected the lettering to carry
The date of the gift, a kind of christening:
This is more like the plate on a coffin.

Louisa Catherine Smith could not be light.
Far more than a maiden name
Was cancelled by him on the first night.

I believe he cannot have known your touch
Like this instrument—for clearly
John Charles did not hold with fingering—

Which is obviously a lady's:
The sound-box trim as a girl in stays,
The neck right for the smallest span.

Did you even keep track of it as a wife?
Do you know the man who has it now
Is giving it the time of its life?

NIGHT DRIVE

The smells of ordinariness
Were new on the night drive through France:
Rain and hay and woods on the air
Made warm draughts in the open car.

Signposts whitened relentlessly.
Montreuil, Abbéville, Beauvais
Were promised, promised, came and went,
Each place granting its name's fulfilment.

A combine groaning its way late
Bled seeds across it work-light.
A forest fire smouldered out.
One by one small cafés shut.

I thought of you continuously
A thousand miles south where Italy
Laid its loin to France on the darkened sphere.
Your ordinariness was renewed there.

AT ARDBOE POINT

Right along the lough shore
A smoke of flies
Drifts thick in the sunset.

They come shattering daintily
Against the windscreen,
The grill and bonnet whisper

At their million collisions:
It is to drive through
A hail of fine chaff.

Yet we leave no clear wake
For they open and close on us
As the air opens and closes.

To-night when we put out our light
To kiss between sheets
Their just audible siren will go

Outside the window,
Their invisible veil
Weakening the moonlight still further

And the walls will carry a rash
Of them, a green pollen.
They'll have infiltrated our clothes by morning.

If you put one under a lens
You'd be looking at a pumping body
With such outsize beaters for wings

That this visitation would seem
More drastic than Pharaoh's—
I'm told they're mosquitoes

But I'd need forests and swamps
To believe it
For these are our innocent, shuttling

Choirs, dying through
Their own live empyrean, troublesome only
As the last veil on a dancer.

RELIC OF MEMORY

The lough waters
Can petrify wood:
Old oars and posts
Over the years
Harden their grain,
Incarcerate ghosts

Of sap and season.
The shallows lap
And give and take—
Constant ablutions,
Such drowning love
Stun a stake

To stalagmite.
Dead lava,
The cooling star,
Coal and diamond
Or sudden birth
Of burnt meteor

Are too simple,
Without the lure
That relic stored.
A piece of stone
On the shelf at school,
Oatmeal coloured.

A LOUGH NEAGH SEQUENCE

for the fishermen

1. UP THE SHORE

I

The lough will claim a victim every year.
It has virtue that hardens wood to stone.
There is a town sunk beneath its water.
It is the scar left by the Isle of Man.

II

At Toomebridge where it sluices towards the sea
They've set new gates and tanks against the flow.
From time to time they break the eels' journey
And lift five hundred stone in one go.

III

But up the shore in Antrim and Tyrone
There is a sense of fair play in the game.
The fishermen confront them one by one
And sail miles out, and never learn to swim.

IV

'We'll be the quicker going down', they say—
And when you argue there are no storms here,
That one hour floating's sure to land them safely—
'The lough will claim a victim every year.'

A gland agitating
mud two hundred miles in-
land, a scale of water
on water working up
estuaries, he drifted
into motion half-way
across the Atlantic,
sure as the satellite's
insinuating pull
in the ocean, as true
to his orbit.
                    Against
ebb, current, rock, rapids
a muscled icicle
that melts itself longer
and fatter, he buries
his arrival beyond
light and tidal water,
investing silt and sand
with a sleek root. By day
only the drainmaker's
spade or the mud paddler
can make him abort. Dark
delivers him hungering
down each undulation.

39

3. BAIT

Lamps dawdle in the field at midnight.
Three men follow their nose in the grass
The lamps' beam their prow and compass.

The bucket's handle better not clatter now:
Silence and curious light gather bait.
Nab him, but wait

For the first shrinking, tacky on the thumb.
Let him re-settle backwards in his tunnel.
Then draw steady and he'll come.

Among the millions whorling their mud coronas
Under dewlapped leaf and bowed blades
A few are bound to be rustled in these might raids,

Innocent ventilators of the ground
Making the globe a perfect fit,
A few are bound to be cheated of it

When lamps dawdle in the field at midnight,
When fishers need a garland for the bay
And have him, where he needs to come, out of the clay.

4. SETTING

I

A line goes out of sight and out of mind
Down to the soft bottom of silt and sand
Past the indifferent skill of the hunting hand.

A bouquet of small hooks coiled in the stern
Is being paid out, back to its true form,
Until the bouquet's hidden in the worm.

The boat rides forward where the line slants back.
The oars in their locks go round and round.
The eel describes his arcs without a sound.

II

The gulls fly and umbrella overhead,
Treading air as soon as the line runs out,
Responsive acolytes above the boat.

Not sensible of any *kyrie*,
The fishers, who don't know and never try,
Pursue the work in hand as destiny.

They clear the bucket of the last chopped worms,
Pitching them high, good riddance, earthy shower.
The gulls encompass them before the water.

5. LIFTING

They're busy in a high boat
That stalks towards Antrim, the power cut.
The line's a filament of smut

Drawn hand over fist
Where every three yards a hook's missed
Or taken (and the smut thickens, wrist-

Thick, a flail
Lashed into the barrel
With one swing). Each eel

Comes aboard to this welcome:
The hook left in gill or gum,
It's slapped into the barrel numb

But knits itself, four-ply,
With the furling, slippy
Haul, a knot of back and pewter belly

That stays continuously one
For each catch they fling in
Is sucked home like lubrication.

And wakes are enwound as the catch
On the morning water: which
Boat was which?

And when did this begin?
This morning, last year, when the lough first spawned?
The crews will answer, 'Once the season's in.'

6. THE RETURN

In ponds, drains, dead canals
she turns her head back,
older now, following
whim deliberately
till she's at sea in grass
and damned if she'll turn so
it's new trenches, sunk pipes,
swamps, running streams, the lough
the river. Her stomach
shrunk, she exhilarates
in mid-water. Its throbbing
is speed through days and weeks.

Who knows now if she knows
her depth or direction;
she's passed Malin and
Tory, silent, wakeless,
a wisp, a wick that is
its own taper and light
through the weltering dark.
Where she's lost once she lays
ten thousand feet down in
her origins. The current
carries slicks of orphaned spawn.

7. VISION

Unless his hair was fine-combed
The lice, they said, would gang up
Into a mealy rope
And drag him, small, dirty, doomed

Down to the water. He was
Cautious then in riverbank
Fields. Thick as a birch trunk
That cable flexed in the grass

Every time the wind passed. Years
Later in the same fields
He stood at night when eels
Moved through the grass like hatched fears

Towards the water. To stand
In one place as the field flowed
Past, a jellied road,
To watch the eels crossing land

Re-wound his world's live girdle.
Phosphorescent, sinewed slime
Continued at his feet. Time
Confirmed the horrid cable.

THE GIVEN NOTE

On the most westerly Blasket
In a dry-stone hut
He got this air out of the night.

Strange noises were heard
By others who followed, bits of a tune
Coming in on loud weather

Though nothing like melody.
He blamed their fingers and ear
As unpractised, their fiddling easy

For he had gone alone into the island
And brought back the whole thing.
The house throbbed like his full violin.

So whether he calls it spirit music
Or not, I don't care. He took it
Out of wind off mid-Atlantic.

Still he maintains, from nowhere.
It comes off the bow gravely,
Rephrases itself into the air.

WHINLANDS

All year round the whin
Can show a blossom or two
But it's in full bloom now.
As if the small yolk stain

From all the birds' eggs in
All the nests of the spring
Were spiked and hung
Everywhere on bushes to ripen.

Hills oxidize gold.
Above the smoulder of green shoot
And dross of dead thorns underfoot
The blossoms scald.

Put a match under
Whins, they go up of a sudden.
They make no flame in the sun
But a fierce heat tremor

Yet incineration like that
Only takes the thorn.
The tough sticks don't burn,
Remain like bone, charred horn.

Gilt, jaggy, springy, frilled
This stunted, dry richness
Persists on hills, near stone ditches,
Over flintbed and battlefield.

THE PLANTATION

Any point in that wood
Was a centre, birch trunks
Ghosting your bearings,
Improvising charmed rings

Wherever you stopped.
Though you walked a straight line
It might be a circle you travelled
With toadstools and stumps

Always repeating themselves.
Or did you re-pass them?
Here were bleyberries quilting the floor,
The black char of a fire

And having found them once
You were sure to find them again.
Someone had always been there
Though always you were alone.

Lovers, birdwatchers,
Campers, gipsies and tramps
Left some trace of their trades
Or their excrement.

Hedging the road so
It invited all comers
To the hush and the mush
Of its whispering treadmill,

Its limits defined,
So they thought, from outside.
They must have been thankful
For the hum of the traffic

If they ventured in
Past the picnickers' belt
Or began to recall
Tales of fog on the mountains.

You had to come back
To learn how to lose yourself,
To be pilot and stray—witch,
Hansel and Gretel in one.

SHORELINE

Turning a corner, taking a hill
In County Down, there's the sea
Sidling and settling to
The back of a hedge. Or else

A grey bottom with puddles
Dead-eyed as fish.
Haphazard tidal craters march
The corn and the grazing.

All round Antrim and westward
Two hundred miles at Moher
Basalt stands to.
Both ocean and channel

Froth at the black locks
On Ireland. And strands
Take hissing submissions
Off Wicklow and Mayo.

Take any minute. A tide
Is rummaging in
At the foot of all fields,
All cliffs and shingles.

Listen. Is it the Danes,
A black hawk bent on the sail?
Or the chinking Normans?
Or currachs hopping high

On to the sand?
Strangford, Arklow, Carrickfergus,
Belmullet and Ventry
Stay, forgotten like sentries.

BANN CLAY

Labourers pedalling at ease
Past the end of the lane
Were white with it. Dungarees
And boots wore its powdery stain.

All day in open pits
They loaded on to the bank
Slabs like the squared-off clots
Of a blue cream. Sunk

For centuries under the grass
It baked white in the sun,
Relieved its hoarded waters
And began to ripen.

It underruns the valley,
The first slow residue
Of a river finding its way.
Above it, the webbed marsh is new,

Even the clutch of Mesolithic
Flints. Once, cleaning a drain
I shovelled up livery slicks
Till the water gradually ran

Clear on its old floor.
Under the humus and roots
This smooth weight. I labour
Towards it still. It holds and gluts.

BOGLAND

for T. P. Flanagan

We have no prairies
To slice a big sun at evening—
Everywhere the eye concedes to
Encroaching horizon,

Is wooed into the cyclops' eye
Of a tarn. Our unfenced country
Is bog that keeps crusting
Between the sights of the sun.

They've taken the skeleton
Of the Great Irish Elk
Out of the peat, set it up
An astounding crate full of air.

Butter sunk under
More than a hundred years
Was recovered salty and white.
The ground itself is kind, black butter

Melting and opening underfoot,
Missing its last definition
By millions of years.
They'll never dig coal here,

Only the waterlogged trunks
Of great firs, soft as pulp.
Our pioneers keep striking
Inwards and downwards,

Every layer they strip
Seems camped on before.
The bogholes might be Atlantic seepage.
The wet centre is bottomless.